DR. PIERRE F. WALTER

BASICS OF
CAREER DESIGN

Opening Inner Space

"Articles Series"

ISBN 978-1-468118-67-4

Contact Information Dr. Pierre F. Walter

publisher@sirius-c-publishing.com

About Dr. Pierre F. Walter

http://drpfw.info

Quotation Suggestion

Pierre F. Walter, *Basics of Career Design: Opening Inner Space*, Newark: Sirius-C Media Galaxy LLC, 2011

About the Author

Pierre F. Walter is an author, international lawyer, researcher, corporate trainer, and lecturer. After finalizing studies in German Law, International Law and *European integration* with diplomas obtained in 1981 through 1983, he graduated in December 1987 at the Law Faculty of the University of Geneva as *Docteur en Droit* in international law.

The doctorate was funded by scholarships from the *Swiss Institute of Comparative Law*, Lausanne, and from the *University of Geneva*, as well as a Fulbright Travel Grant for an assistantship with Professor Louis B. Sohn at *UGA Law School Department of International Law*, Athens, Georgia, USA, in 1985. Pierre F. Walter also served as a research assistant to *Freshfields, Bruckhaus, Deringer,* Cologne, Germany in 1983 and to *Lalive Lawyers,* Geneva, in 1987.

Pierre F. Walter writes and lectures in English, German and French languages; he has written *more than ten thousand pages* embracing all literary genres, including *novels, short stories, film scripts, essays, selfhelp books, monographs* and extended *book reviews*. Also a pianist and composer, he has realized 40 CDs with *jazz, newage* and *relaxation music*.

Pierre F. Walter's professional publications span the domains *International Law, Criminal Law, Holistic Science, Psychology, Education, Shamanism, Ecology, Spirituality, Quantum Physics, Systems Theory, Natural Healing, Peace Research, Personal Growth, Selfhelp* and *Consciousness Research*. 110 Book Reviews, thirty-eight audio books and more than hundred video lectures were realized in the years 2005-2010. Besides, Pierre F. Walter is author and editor of *Great Minds Series*, which features scientists, artists and authors of genius from Leonardo to Fritjof Capra.

Pierre F. Walter publishes via his Delaware firm *Sirius-C Media Galaxy LLC* and the imprints IPUBLICA and Sirius-C Media (SCM).

For Nelson

CONTENTS

INTRODUCTION

The Fool's Voyage

Your career can be compared to a *voyage* in space and time, the space and the time of your life. Both inspired writers such as Joseph Campbell and brilliant psychiatrists such as Carl-Gustav Jung compared our professional career with following an inner call, bringing about a state of bliss, or fulfilling our higher destiny. Career consultants such as Laurence G. Boldt call our professional voyage our *life's work*, thus expressing the uniqueness and importance of realizing the best of our talents and capacities in our work.[1] We could also say that giving birth to, and incarnate, our life's mission is an opportunity put in our cradle that we surely should not miss. And yet this is something we do not generally learn in school and if parents are not mature enough to be mirrors to their children, the latter are at pains to recognize and nurture their unique talents and gifts.

There are methods and techniques that help us finding out about who we are and what we are to do in this world. These methods range from simply asking ourselves, a tech-

---

[1] See my review of all of Boldt's books in Pierre F. Walter, *110 Book Reviews (2010)*. See also details of his books in the annexed Bibliography.

nique that Laurence G. Boldt promotes and applies to more complex strategies, group interactions and self-finding therapies. You can also use more esoteric techniques such as astrology, numerology, consulting a medium or using divination such as the Tarot, the Runes or the I Ching.[2]

This article, then, presents some of those techniques that may appeal to those of you who, like myself during my childhood and youth, are so sadly alienated from their true being that they would not be able to tap into their true potential by just asking a question to themselves. For me, it was *potential astrology* that brought the solution and showed the way to go.

Excited about the perspectives of a career as spiritual teacher and counselor that was traced out in my birth chart, I was honest enough to admit that I was suffering from a certain amount of neurotic symptoms that made it extremely difficult to do the necessary changes without competent help. Thus, I engaged in a hypnotherapy that helped me integrate all I was forced to split off, during my childhood and youth, from my true personality, my soul and my feelings. During this therapy that I completed with private work on my *inner selves*, I became painfully aware of the fact that I had been living an extremely residual existence, an existence of utter self-denial while on the outside level I had been well adjusted

---

[2] See Pierre F. Walter, *Divination Basics (2011)* and *Taoism and the I Ching (2011)*.

and succeeded to become an international lawyer, doctor of law and legal advisor.[3]

In this article I will thus mention some useful strategies that may help you open this space that you may still ignore and that you cannot simply access using your wake consciousness because during years and years of survival, when you were a child, you had to repress certain intuitions about yourself and your life, and certain feelings, because you were not accepted as you were, but as the person you *faked* you were. This *fake existence* as it were was not your choice, but a necessity for you to survive in an environment, be it family, be it school, or both, that you felt was hostile to your true existence and what you most wanted to be. Thus, what you did was to repress your true self, your *me*, and create an artificial mask, a *fake-me*, that you put in place as a protective shield and that helped you to survive that hostile childhood.

I intently say *survive* because that's what it is. You were not living this childhood, but you lived *through it* to get it behind your back as soon as possible; for *living* it, truly you would have needed to be accepted for what you were because life requires a certain amount of autonomy. If autonomy is denied to us as children, our courage to realize our innermost desires is thwarted and our will is bent.[4] And without

---

[3] See Pierre F. Walter, *The Inner Journey, Scholarly Article (2011)*.

[4] See my audio book *Eight Patterns of Living (2010)*, where the *Autonomy Pattern* is the first of these eight patterns that I found to be existent with most tribal populations.

courage and will, without knowing who we are, how can we ever achieve to find and realize the career of our heart?

In my experience this fate is even more often experienced with boys than with girls, especially when the constellation is *single female parent left alone by her husband raises a single male child*. In that constellation which was the one I myself experienced as a child, the amount of alienation a boy may be facing to go through can be extreme. Females, in my experience, have an easier connection to the ground, the earth, the roots of their being, than males. This is perhaps not biologically so but it is certainly culturally so, because it has been so since the beginning of patriarchy and thus since about five thousand years. Thus, *a single girl being raised by a single father* does in no way face the same psychic constellation as a single boy raised by a single mother.

I have laid out the deeper intricacies of such personal fates and destinies in other publications, and will therefore restrict myself here to a general overview over methods that can help us in our quest for self.[5]

There are three different kinds of methodologies: *therapeutic methods, shamanic methods* and *divinatory methods*. Regarding therapeutic methods, I am going to give you an overview over classical *Freudian psychotherapy, Transactional Analysis (TA), Hypnotherapy* and Bioenergetics; regarding divinatory methods, I will shortly present you *Potential Astrology*, the *Tarot* and the *I Ching*. In addition, there are teachings that have not de-

---

[5] See Pierre F. Walter, *The Idiot Guide to Soul Power (2010)* and *The Idiot Guide to Love (2010)*.

veloped precise methods for finding your life's work, but that help you finding out *who you are*, and thus help you gain more *self-knowledge.*

Please be aware that without self-knowledge, without knowing who you are and why you have come into this existence, you cannot really find out what your life's mission is. Both quests are interconnected and I would say that the spiritual quest, the quest for self-knowledge, is the more basic one. These teachings, that I will be mentioning shortly, are shamanic teachings or generally religious teachings with an emphasis on the individual soul and destiny. Please note that these teachings are not at all moralistic but scientific in a sense that they try to look at life with what in Zen is called a *beginner's mind.*

When you inquire in European mythology you become early aware that it's marked by murder and again murder. I shall not indulge in recounting senseless murder stories that some psychologists take for the blank truth, but just give a short sketch. Up to the reader to inquire further, using Wikipedia or other sources of knowledge.

I have said my last word on European murder mythology in my audio book *The Lunar Bull (2010)*, the text of which is published in my *Idiot Guide to Consciousness (2010)*, Chapter Four (The Spiritual Laws of Matriarchy). You may want to check these sources out.

For all those *joyful idealists* who adore and worship Greek and Roman cultures, among them being many boylovers and homosexuals, I can only say that these cultures were decadent no lesser than ours. Only look at the sordid ways that

Socrates was persecuted and put to death, to have one of many examples of the pretended 'liberty' and 'democracy' of ancient Greek culture! With our lauded 'worldwide democracy', it's exactly the same, it slaughters the innocent marginal lover who engages in a consenting embrace with an underage girl and empowers the greatest abusers, in the form of mafias and weapon-smuggling and drug-trading governments and their secret services to levels never before known in the entire human history.

By the way, the often-praised *boylove* was an idealist movement that was restricted to nobility, while that very nobility practiced slavery and violent warfare, the relegation of women to the wedlock, and the total lack of protection for little girls in a society that I can only name as 'totally homosexual' in all senses of the word. And that was even worse with the Romans where only the male had all the power and where females were having about the power as today within fundamentalist Islamic regimes. It is confirmed today by violence research that these factors suffice to qualify any given society as 'highly violent'.

We see currently the same trend. Our Western society is 'homosexualizing' itself with every year to come, a phenomenon that always goes along with a tightening of the laws, with draconian punishments, witch-hunts, spectacular scapegoat trials where people are virtually 'slaughtered' for the perverse indulgence of the mob, just as during the *Roman Games*, and a general fascism that veils the essential and basically runs on hypocrisy as the slime that snakes and snails the whole societal building.

I will not take a decadent culture that has lost any balance between *yang* and *yin* values as a denominator for our collective psyche as Carl Jung did it, while he relegated the female to the *anima* role. Joseph Campbell was more precise in this point, calling the female principle under patriarchy the 'counterplayer' in our psychic setup. *Counterplayer* sounds good and strong, and it empowers the female principle in the sense that while it's on the level of the unconscious, it contains real power.[6]

Let me explain more in detail what I mean. In a natural society, men by and large love women and women by and large love men. This doesn't exclude that there may be a small percentage of homosexuality, sadism, pedophilia, nepiophilia, zoophilia and other *paraphilias*, perhaps around 1 to 3%.[7]

Such a society will however not persecute those sexual minorities but tolerate them as the 'marginal' freaks, the harlequins, the bizarre folk, the black-and-beautiful sheep. It will by no means be violent toward them, while they may be ridiculed in public at times, without however being harmed in any way.

Now, what is the result of this integrative attitude? The result is that a social persecution of those minorities and thereby, a state of *civil war*, will not arise. Such a society can

---

[6] See Joseph Campbell, *Occidental Mythology (1991)*, p. 70. See also Pierre F. Walter, *Joseph Campbell and the Lunar Bull (2010)*.

[7] To learn more about sexual paraphilias, please peruse Pierre F. Walter, *The Idiot Guide to Emotions (2010)* and *The Idiot Guide to Love (2010)* as well as my monograph and *Energy Science and Vibrational Healing (2010)*.

thus endure as it is overall *integrative* and *cohesive*. This is valid for most tribal cultures around the world and the early matriarchies, among them *Minoan Civilization* as perhaps the highest development of the *integrative social principle.*

In such a society, sexual minorities are considered equal when applying for a job. To give an example. Just recently, in Thailand, a new domestic airline opened its doors, and it hired transsexuals as stewardesses. Not all of them are *ladyboys*, but well about one third. The general manager of the airline explained in a television interview that one hundred transsexuals had applied for the job, and that those few who had been hired, had been screened for one entire day, to make sure they really had a female appearance, female manners and the ability to work well with the other real females in the crew.

Now, let us see how the picture looks like in a culture where pleasure was perverted into violence through *denial and moralism*, as for example in an early patriarchal invader tribe. In such a cultural setting, which is remote from the rules of nature, and typically is out to *control and dominate nature*, men by and large love men and women by and large love women. However, this fact is veiled behind a strong rhetoric of 'cultural garbage' in the form of *hypocrisy* that puts up moralistic rules that hide the reality of how people relate to each other on the erotic plane.

In fact, there will be large-scale *sadism* in all erotic relations. This leads to men professing to not only love but have Don Juan relations with many women, while they are in fact homosexual and women professing to not only love but have

Nymphomaniac relations with many men, while they are in fact Lesbian. In general, this leads to a considerable percentage of homosexuality, sadism, pedophilia, nepiophilia, zoophilia and other *paraphilias*, perhaps around 10 to 30% of the society, thus about ten times higher as in natural cultures.[8]

Such a society will ruthlessly persecute those sexual minorities, and not tolerate them as 'marginal' freaks, but call them *offenders*, criminals and system enemies, if not sexual terrorists, and will try to completely annihilate them through Euthanasia laws, as they were practiced in the Nazi regime and other fascist regimes in the past. Such as system will be setup to not only harm these individuals, but to completely eradicate them through large-scale *planned murder and genocide.*

Now, what is the result of this disintegrative attitude? The result is that there will be large-scale social and legal persecution of those minorities and thereby, a state of *civil war*, in the long run. Such a society can thus *not* endure as it is overall *disintegrative* and *abrasive.*

Such a society will thus breed violence through its intolerance to sexual diversity, and through the persecution of those who defy the norm, and even prior to that, by the very fact of erecting a sexual norm. In fact, by nature, there are no sexual norms. This is simply so. It's the very fact that control was put over *self-regulation*, or culture over nature, or else

---

[8] Please note that I am speculating here. The percentage may be lower or higher, but that doesn't change the point I am making here, as I am only showing the structural connections. It would need much further research to present a verified theory, of course. By the way, I doubt that such a research is possible at all, as so much of this information is hidden and would need to be digged out from underground sources of knowledge.

conditioning over carefreeness that this state of *perversion* from the natural norm was brought about. You can also put it in the short form of neurosis and the blockage of bioenergy being considered superior to self-regulation and the streaming of the bioenergy.

Why do I mention this in a career guide? Well, these factors have a real impact upon your career success because we are all different, and there is no such thing as 'absolute normality' in the human psychosexual setup. Hence, if you feel you are different, or 'too different', and you have nobody to coach or help you to build a stable identity, you will have hardships to be accepted in the corporate world.

Now, it is obvious that we are the latter, not the former culture, as our present society originates from the violent patriarchal tribes that massacred the Minoan and other matriarchal cultures who practiced *erotic intelligence*, to erect stupidity as the norm. Let us assume that many of us understand this cultural madness and want to get back at natural sanity, okay? Then, of course, we must ask what is the way to go? Is that question easy to answer? Let us see.

Let us have a deeper look at the factors that we realistically could change and that have to do with our 'mythology of violence', so to speak. You got a glimpse what this *murder mythology* is actually based upon, so we only need to find the antidote to those ingredients.

You can make up your own theory of course, but please for a moment listen to what I have to say as somebody who researched for twenty-seven years on human emotions and sexuality. In my view, what we have to do is to rebuild emotional and erotic intelligence in our new generations, as a matter of an urgent social policy to prevent social and sexual violence in our next generation, for the karma is very queer. If we want to be effective, we need to take a holistic and integrative approach to *human emotions and sexuality* and change the pattern right at its root.

And in this endeavor, the old murder mythology cannot help us. We need to forge a new mythology, we have to restart from scratch, or we will perish. And of course, when I say we have to forge a new mythology, that means we have to change our consciousness, as these archetypes are well written into our collective unconscious, as Carl Jung found. But even though this is a huge change, we can effect it.

This is how it is on the collective level. But on the personal, individual level, the process also needs to be put in place. This means for you, as you want to start your career in the best possible condition, you need to go through this process yourself, as a person and member of this society.

What does that imply? It implies that you build conscious awareness of these factors as you cannot escape the society in which you live, except you are going to leave your country and go to live in an exotic, and erotically more intelligent culture than yours. The obstacles to such a way are obvious. To just mention one of those obstacles. Most of these societies are shamanic cultures and have a rather low technological standard. Hence, they do not have any or only rudimentary corporate work platforms. Hence, when you have finished college, what you need in the first place is that opportunity to enter the corporate world as soon as possible, and as young as possible. This is how the system works, as going up the career ladder is a very gradual process, and cannot be forced. Those structures need to be in place before you can even start. The problem with exotic cultures is that they do not have those structures in place. You may go backpacking there and returning with some new insights, but making your career in any of those cultures is really quite difficult, also from a language point of view.

What, then, is the way to go? It is of course all up to your own perception and decision-making but to generalize, I would say that the best option is to stay within your culture and make your career there, but without conforming with all that this culture requires from its citizens. Sigmund Freud is credited to have called this approach, as a novelty insight, the 'reality principle', as opposed to the *pleasure principle*. Without going into the details of psychoanalysis now, let me confess that I do not entirely agree with Freud on this matter. I do believe that *pleasure is a necessity in life,* and that real fulfillment in your career can only be found when you do experience pleasure when you do your work. Having studied the lives of many a genius, being in art of science, I have seen clearly that they are derive an enormous amount of pleasure from their work.[9] In more general terms, many psychiatrists and psychologists agree that the way to be successful is about half way between total conformation to the system, and total abstention from it. In other words, you need to be flexible and

---

[9] See Pierre F. Walter, *Do You Love Einstein?, Creative Insights into Perennial Wisdom, Human Genius and the Quantum Field,* Monograph *(2010).*

in addition affirmative toward your own difference, whatever it happens to be. To give an example, the Canadian pianist Glenn Gould (1932-1982) who was extraordinarily successful in his overall pianistic career, had to come to grips with his difference in style and his so-called 'extra-musical behaviors' (such as sitting very low on a special foldable chair he carries with him, playing with crossed legs, humming, singing or conducting) that in the words of his psychiatrist were defense mechanisms against his enormous stage anxiety.[10] At the beginning of his career, he was sometimes harshly admonished by critics, and even ridiculed. Yet the secret of his success is that he ultimately was sticking to his style instead of giving up on it, to imitate any other style of any other successful pianist.

In an important book on career design, entitled *Tactics*, by Edward de Bono, a thorough research on highly successful people revealed that it is conducive to success to hold on to your own style, instead of copying the style of any other person who is successful in his life and career. Hence the need for you to develop your own style and at the same time some firmness to resist when others, be it friends, tell you to change your style. You can realize only the latent gifts and talents that are within you, not the ones of another person.[11]

---

[10] See *Life and Times* on Glenn Gould. See also glenngould.ca

[11] Edward de Bono, *Tactics: The Art and Science of Success (1985/1993).*

BECOMING AN INDIVIDUAL

The Journey to Self

The *Tree of Life* is different from the Pedigree or Genea-
logical Tree. To walk into your own life basically implies to
leave home, and to make the psychological cut with the matrix.
For this to happen, we have to go through a whole process of
identity building that commences as early as in babyhood.
Building identity is coupled with building autonomy.

Liz Greene & Juliet Sharman-Burke write in their en-
lightening study *The Mythic Journey (2000)*:

Liz Greene & Juliet Sharman-Burke

There is a mysterious impulse in all of us to become
ourselves – unique and defined individuals apart from
the family bonds, partnerships and community life
which give us a feeling of identity. But, as myth tells us,
the process of becoming an individual is a hard and
sometimes painful one. It involves not only a willing-
ness to meet the inner and outer challenges that test
our strength, but also a capacity to stand alone and
endure the envy or hostility of those us who have not
yet begun this journey towards selfhood. Myth presents us with stories about how hard it is to leave home
and what kind of dragons we must encounter and fight
in our struggle towards autonomy. Not least, mythic
tales also reveal the profound importance of a sense of
personal purpose and meaning – perhaps the deepest
mystery imbedded in our efforts to become what we
truly are. We may not always recognize the degree to
which we have avoided the challenge of individuality
and the everyday ways in which we betray our most
heartfelt values in order to feel we belong. In these
spheres, myths can offer not only insight, but also the
reassurance that self-development is not necessarily the
same thing as selfishness. We cannot really offer to
others what we have not yet developed within
ourselves.[12]

---

[12] Liz Greene & Juliet Sharman-Burke, *The Mythic Journey (2000)*, p. 73.

Our present social and educational system makes us believe that there are standard truths for all of us, standard values, standard forms of behavior and a standardized morality framework for all of us.

A natural science that was deeply alienated from spiritual truth and whose main advocate was Charles Darwin has led many to simply compare humans to the animal race and to deduct social, political and psychological conclusions from such a haphazard premise. The fact that we all got two arms and two legs does not mean that we can compare human beings with each other on a soul level.

If we could, it would be easy and practical to work out standards for self-improvement and promote them worldwide in schools, universities and the media.

I do not say that this idea is nonsense per se. In the contrary, I am the first to advocate it and I do work hard for its realization. But only if the primary condition is met. This condition is that the methods taught are only pathways to guide people toward *their own inner guru*, and not to establish the ultimate Big Brother Gurus & Co. multinational.

The only wisdom you can learn is the one you have got already, that is contained in your *continuum*, your own inner space, your timeless soul, your potential. All wisdom, all knowledge that we can find, we knew it already before, and if we wish, we can find it again. I think we all have gone, as humans, through the loss of connectedness with our true source.

From this experience of loss we keep a deep-down memory, somewhere in our collective unconscious. Based upon this memory and the depression and loneliness that followed, we have developed a feeling of anticipation, a deep anxiety regarding the lost knowledge. This is why many of us today still reject what they call esoteric knowledge or make it down as superstition or imagination.

Life is our own creation at every infinitesimal point of the lifeline. The lifeline itself has no beginning and no end and therefore is more appropriately described as the *circle-of-life*, or even more accurately as the *spiral-of-life*. There is no doubt about our impact upon the invisible threads out of which the web of life is woven. However, the depressed and alienated masses tend to believe that there is, if ever, only negligible individual control over life and that life is *per se* destined to be this or that way, according to some mysterious heavenly plan. In reality, there simply is no such plan. It is interesting to see to what extent this wrong presumption contributes to the dullness of the ignorant masses.

Contemplating the power of nature, of creation, how can one associate anything but *freedom* with the fundamental force from which sprang all the thousand things? This force has created unlimited freedom and power. However, humans have limited it to the tiny stupid thing that they have made out of life and that they use to call *their* life. They talk of *my* life and *your* life, as if we individually owned life, as if life could be *owned* at all. Only things can be owned but life is not a thing, but a dynamic, energetic process – a cosmic dance.

Only utter ignorance about the very roots of life could bring about the present state of affairs among us humans, this desperate dependency and passivity of humans worldwide. Of course, we are very busy imitating others and in that many people find their shallow satisfaction. It is a lack of energy, of commitment to ourselves and our individual, very specific mission that makes us comply with the baseline of living and transforms us into bad copies of ourselves.

Few people live original lives, *first-hand lives*. Compared with the masses of imitators and robots that run around on this globe, these people represent a tiny minority. And if you look close at them you find out quickly that they are always the contradictors, the ones who try to do things differently, the ones who are not easily satisfied, not easily duped into some petty mediocre thing, be it a job or a partner or a million in the lottery. Their value system is strangely different from the one most people have blindly adopted. When they were children, they were keen, very curious, sometimes excessively inquisitive, yet not out of low intention but from a deep thirst for human experience and interest in the human soul. In school, or more generally, in systems, educational, military or otherwise, they are the big or small disturbers, the ones who never fit in, the ones who won't comply with most of the rules, the ones also who spontaneously create different rules that, typically, function better than the rules they broke.

I do not say that you have to become a rule-breaker in order to get to know your original self, while rule-breaking at times *does* trigger a personal path of self-perfection. I do say, however, that in order to get in touch with your own originality, you have to become acutely aware of all the influences you are exposed to at any moment of your life. Why? Because there are influences that are beneficial for your growth and there are others that are harmful for it or that for the least are going to retard it. The art of life is all about being able to *distinguish* the latter influences from the former. Some authors and gurus require an inner purification before they admit that our soul can grow and develop. However, this means to put a time element in something that is beyond or outside of time.

Matters concerning the soul or our higher self are outside the time-space continuum. If we assume that growth processes on this level can only take place after going through a sort of soul graduation, we assemble events on a timeline that have no place there.

It seems smarter to admit that the very process of growing implies in itself a purification of old soul content. There is probably, without our knowing of it, a continuous process of renewal going on in the soul. In addition, it seems more effective to think in terms of evolution than in terms of purification. Purification deals with the past, evolution focuses on the future. If I want to ride a bicycle or a car and watch the road too closely, I am accident-prone. I ride safely if I gaze within a farther distance.

The same is true for personal evolution. Directed, voluntary progress is possible only if there is vision, and a vision that heads farther into the future than just tomorrow or next week. True vision is created by your *higher self*, after deep relaxation, by centering within and by accepting your uniqueness. Many people, especially from the older generation, find it against the rules of good taste to focus upon themselves, to do self-improvement or generally to bestow attention on themselves. Many of them carry along deep guilt feelings from childhood, often having suffered mistreatment and neglect in their early years. As a result, they tend to block off when they are asked to take care of themselves. They may indulge in a good deal of social help for others, assist in welfare projects, or be otherwise useful to the community. More often than not, their self-neglect ends with a cancer or some other violent disease that crowns the big *sacrifice* they wanted to offer with their life!

We cannot be ultimately useful if we regard ourselves as useless. We cannot bestow loving attention upon others if we do not give it to us first. True religion, in the sense of the word, begins with taking care of self and soul.[13] This is not a *religion of egotism* as you may haphazardly consider it, but the only true religion. We do never know others good enough to judge their spiritual views, needs and belongings. We are all on different levels of evolution and different spheres of existence and belong to different soul groups and energy fields; and we all have had different former lives, incarnations and challenges, and we all carry different visions about our individual evolution and the evolution of our clan or race. It is this difference about our soul origins that makes us so helpless when we talk about what we call *spiritual matters*. Have you ever observed that people talk on different levels of consciousness when they discuss about what is called *spirituality?* The true lover of truth does not make a distinction between

---

[13] See Thomas Moore, *Care of the Soul: A Guide for Cultivating Depth and Sacredness in Everyday Life (1994).*

spiritual and non-spiritual matters since this distinction is artificial and without value. For the spiritually minded being, *everything is spiritual*. For the materialistically minded individual, *everything is material*. Life is a whole process and every attempt to divide it up, to section it, to dissect it into various parts is detrimental to grasping its perfume.

Once you understand the wholeness and holiness of life, you understand your own wholeness and holiness. Then, you are on the path of success and your career shall unfold in conformity with your greater life cycle.

ADAM & EVE

Leaving Paradise

Metaphorically, we can compare symbiosis with paradise. Adam and Eve had to leave paradise – why? They had to leave paradise for developing their individuality, their autonomy. Paradises are not different from other things in that they, too, have a shadow: positively, they give us the almost complete illusion of security and satisfy all possible desires. But negatively, they are true prisons.

The tree of knowledge was forbidden in paradise to Adam and Eve – and we must add, *even* in paradise! Or, more clearly put, it was forbidden to them *because* they lived in paradise. To live with their full potential, Adam and Eve had to follow the wisdom of the serpent. Eating the apple, they knew each other as man and woman: they got to know about their sexual identity. It was also their discovery of sexuality since the Bible uses the old expression to 'know another' for sexual intercourse.

Through the fact of knowing the other, recognizing the sexual identity of the partner, we get information about our own sexual identity. This is an important truth: love leads to self-knowledge and is a part of our growth process. Without loving others, and I dare to specify, *making love with others*, we will hardly get to know ourselves. Through love we grow, we mature. Leaving paradise is exactly this, leaving the childhood of dependency implying a self-sufficient, narcissistic way of being, and opening up to *true relationship* where every partner is a whole autonomous beings. Love means relating and taking responsibility for one's love choices.

All sentient beings have to leave the nest of paradise. The fetus, decided he to stay in the womb to avoid the trauma of birth, would die right there! Adam and Eve, leaving paradise, survived! Their leaving paradise was a birth, a birth to life on earth, life in a body of flesh, created by desire, an *incarnated* life.

The family tree and the phylogenetic tree both symbolize the nest, the matrix. They are the symbols for the hereditary roots of the person. But they are also prisons and graves for the individual. This truth is pointed out in many religious scriptures and Ramana Maharshi expresses it in the formula that we have to go *beyond the confusion that we are the body*, that we should set aside our unconscious or conscious identification with the body.[14] Once we have found that we are spiritual beings, sparkles of light in a universe of light or planets or stars, as the natives say, we understand that the family is only the nest and as such a kind of springboard which should catapult us into life, into our own life.

---

[14] See Ramana Maharshi, *The Collected Works of Maharshi (2002)*.

GURU & DISCIPLE

The Learning Relation

The true meaning of the guru-disciple relation is often hidden, and in our modern times, it is often profoundly misunderstood. To begin with, such a relationship has nothing to do with what the famous American coach Anthony Robbins sells as 'modeling', which is to more or less clone another person who is very successful, in order to become oneself successful. It is by no means by 'cloning the guru' that one becomes connected with one's own self. It is rather as it is said in Zen that one has to 'kill the Buddha in order to become the Buddha'.

The role of some people we meet in life is to help us detaching from alienating fusion, so that we can build true autonomy. These people who catalyze in us our true desire or mission are healers, therapists or wistful lay persons who help us get free through their love and devotion, and their unselfish understanding and friendship. Often these people went themselves through the problems involved in fusion and have therefore sharpened their awareness. They may have come to the insight that true love is something different from pseudo-symbiotic attachment to others and that love gives freedom, not attachment. Some of these people have little awareness of their role as healers and appear to us in humble appearance or situation, which however does by no means affect the light they bring us.

Inner freedom begins with finding out what we really want, what, in the depth of our heart, we desire to realize, and what is our life's mission. Self-knowledge is the door to inner freedom in that it gives us the tools that lead us out of our labyrinths of *pseudo-symbiosis*. Without knowing who we are we let ourselves over to being guided by others. Such entanglement in the energies outside of the self leads, especially in the spiritual realm, to more or less complete alienation from our own potential of light, riches and abundance.

Self-knowledge opens the door to the treasures of our own light and our own truth which is available to all of us as spiritual beings. But this treasure is in our heart and, with many of us, unfortunately too well protected and therefore buried there. Self-knowledge is a continuous process of self-exploration. It gradually unveils all the secrets of our being and our individuality that will remain untouched by collective religious undertakings.

Self-knowledge leads to comprehending the *relativity of truth* and the incapacity of man to grasp an absolute concept of truth. This limitation of the human existence is inherent in every truth. *Therefore, on the human level all that is objective becomes subjective, because subjectively related!*

There are gurus who reject worldly power while at the same time exerting a much greater power over their followers than the worldly approach would allow. Such opinions are not only not true, they are not only not spiritual, they unveil how power is perceived of by most people, namely a strange, alienating and dominating force that we either reject or eagerly want to acquire.

That is why most people live in an almost paranoid contradiction; while they reject power, they are not aware that they reject their own soul power as well. Doing this, they throw out the baby with the bathwater. And while they want to acquire outside power by all means, they are not aware of the power they possess inside and which, striving for mere outside power, they diminish or smash by non-attention. The result of this strange situation is that both the power-rejecters and the power-seekers are blind to the necessity and the value of power!

The distorted image of their own power potential makes them split the human race into the oppressed or power-rejecters, on one hand, and the oppressors or the power-seekers, on the other. They tend to argue that in life there is only one essential choice to be made: to choose if you want to situate yourself among the oppressed, or losers, rather than switching to the side of the oppressors, or winners. *Tertium non datur.*

Many people unconsciously harbor this kind of an inner program, that is written in the language of either-or options. If I do not want to be poor, I have to become rich. If I do not want to be among the losers, I have to go for becoming a winner. And so on. The blind spot of these philosophies is obviously that they exclude the *tertium*, the third alternative.

In general, when analyzing people with either-or philosophies, we see that they are torn up by fears, that they are rather defensive and that their self-esteem is quite low. If somebody else, a friend for example, tries to put the finger on the wound and tells them about their bias, they react either with aggression or call the friend naive, or else jovially point out that 'unfortunately the world is essentially bad' or 'people are essentially bad' and that therefore one had to make sure to find a place in the sun, cost it what it will.

Now, if we see this clearly, we can approach the problem from a psychological point of view. This allows us to gain insight in the human nature by discarding out quick judgments about what we think or believe human beings are like.

That kind of general judgments are conditioned by our past experiences and hurts. They are highly subjective. True knowledge about the human nature is not abstract and hardly to be gathered other than by passive self-observation.

When we observe the phenomenon of power or what we think it is, both at the outside and inside level, we see that there is something we could identify as *soul power*, and something we could call *worldly power*. Worldly power always is a projection, while soul power is the true power.

What does this mean in detail? Let's go slowly into this, because it is a very complex matter. The danger in this kind of analysis is to jump to conclusions that are conditioned by the past, and by our old convictions and ideas. To approach the problem with a fresh mind means that we try to change our point of departure; it is like changing the observer, to use the terminology of *quantum physics*. This implies that we once again look inside of ourselves in order to see what power really is or how we usually perceive it. If I do this now, supposing that you do it with me, what do I see? I see that with all that I want, with all my desire for fulfillment, for accomplishment, for recognition, for outside riches, I want essentially three things:

> ▸ Live my life without fear;

▸ Live in peace with the world;

▸ Realize love and happiness in my relationships.

When I see now that this is what I really want, what then? Would I not inquire why I experience fear at all? And would I not be astonished why I want to live in peace? Peace – for what? I can't buy anything for that. And why should I realize love and happiness in my relationships? What value has that? Once I have the position that gives me power, once I have the partner that really fulfills me, once I have the car I ever dreamt of and the house that gives me enough space and freedom to feel *at home* – would I not feel satisfied and happy? Why should I question this damn concept of power at all?

Of course, you can refuse looking at it. You are free to do so. But once in a while, these questions tend to come up anyway, if you wish or not, and a *felt sense* of what you really desire comes up as well. And then you are puzzled, because you wonder why you should desire such commonplace childish things as peace or happiness in a world that you think has no place for that.

When we look again, we may stop a moment and see that the world hardly can have a place for that, if we individually do not *give it a place.* The world is at peace. The only creation that is not is the human being. Agreed? What you get to see in our media world is disempowering for the most part. I even go as far as saying that you, in your role as a passive media and information consumer, are *per se disempowered!*

And as long as you are disempowered, your perception of power is distorted.

If you look with this distorted concept inside of you, you see yourself through thick glasses, because your perception is conditioned.

Thus, by meeting the guru, we actually meet our own inner guide, metaphorically incarnated in the guru. And through the guru we do not become like the guru, but more and more ourselves. That is the magic of the guru-disciple relation when it's understood from its origins, and not in its perverted version of *global business guruism.*

In this sense, the guru may be an ordinary person in the eyes of the world, a person from your own country and even your own neighborhood; it can also be a family member, but is often not the father, but an uncle or grandfather. The mythological content in the guru archetype is that it is *self-reflective*, and not dogmatic, sharing knowledge, not imposing knowledge.

It may be easily understood from the foregoing that gurus must have mastered their early hangups in the sense that they must be free of the need for imposing their own story upon their disciples, but are able to see the uniqueness in the disciple, and thus restrain themselves when it goes to sharing their personal story. They know that our personal stories are only the crutches that got us on our own track, and thus they know what counts in life is the *process of becoming* itself, not the becoming as a final goal that serves self-satisfaction.

To get on your own track, you do not need a guru, but it can be helpful in certain situations and especially in bifurcating situations to see oneself mirrored in the compassionate eyes of an experienced guru. It can help avoid mistakes and taking bad routes, if only that, but it is anyway a transforming experience to meet even once a person who has reached the transpersonal state of personal realization. It's a transforming experience!

GLOSSARY

Relevant Terms

Co-Dependence

Parent-child co-dependence frequently if not typically occurs within the *modern nuclear family*. I use the following terms synonymously with co-dependence: co-fusion, secondary fusion, pseudo-symbiosis and symbiotoholism.

Co-dependence is a dependency problem that manifests in the parent-child relation typically for the first time after the critical mother-infant symbiosis, and thus as a general rule after the first eighteen months of the newborn.

What is generally very little known is the fact that even before the completion of the 18th month of the infant, mother and child are interacting in a subtle communication about limits which reveals to what extent the mother is able and willing to give the infant autonomy, or not. This early dialogue, that is most of the time nonverbal, has been found to deeply condition people for their later relational behavior patterns. Causative factors that have been revealed in my own research and the research of other researchers are:

– mother did not really want the child;

– mother is professionally over-engaged, lacking time for the infant;

– lack of healthy physical interaction between parents and child;

– overly strong career focus of parents, leaving child to babysitters;

– insufficient eye contact in the mother-infant relation;

– insufficient or no breast feeding;

– insufficient tactile stimulation of the baby (tactile deprivation);

– shame-based identity of the mother and resulting rejection behavior:

– father left family during pregnancy, after birth or shortly thereafter;

– father, while still part of the family, is as good as never present;

– father refuses to take over an active role in childcare;

– father is abusive toward mother and/or the child, etc.

In other words, co-dependence is a compensation reaction of entangled organisms that tries to heal a split that was caused by a lack of early parent-child intimacy.

The entanglement paradoxically comes about through a *lack of physical closeness,* and of communication, and through a general *tactile deprivation* of the child, and also through non-physical elements such as parents' thoughts constantly focused on money and status or children generally relegated to receiving affection from secondary caretakers, babysitters, house teachers, and the like. The entanglement specifically comes about through the fact of lacking autonomy of the child, and of lacking exposure to experiences and a social life outside of the family. This has been shown with abundant evidence by the long-term research of James W. Prescott, Ashley Montagu, Michel Odent, Frederick Leboyer, Alexander Lowen and others.

The problem of co-dependence is for obvious reasons much more stringent in the individualistic and separative white Western cultures than in highly sociable 'open' societies such as African, South American or Asian cultures. Yet in these cultures today we face the problem in the middle and upper classes as well because they have adopted Western values and a lifestyle that imitates most of the alienated Western behavior models, thereby shunning their own perennial wisdom, that most of their grandparents still are knowledgeable about.

There are many false signals in today's popular culture and vulgarized psychological publications. These false signals lead to parents' becoming more and more insecure as to the role physical affection plays in parenting. This makes that parents are more or less constantly bombarded with ambiguous messages with the result that many of them anxiously retreat physically from their children, thereby inclosing them in atrocious feelings of abandonment, loneliness and despair. As a result of the misguided 1960s American pediatrics, that fostered a physical separation between parents and child which in the meantime is seen as a fundamental error, many of today's parents have never had an affectionate childhood themselves and become dysfunctional parents of their own children. Another important insight about mother-child co-dependence is that it deprives the child, typically the boy, of the time and care needed for developing his true intelligence. Men who grow up entangled with their mothers are caught in a net of stiffening responsibilities, or obligations, or what is felt as such, which impedes them from really thinking of themselves, and minding their own business. The result is that they hardly think their projects through to the end, constantly harassed by their demanding mothers, threatened with love denial or even financial starving in case they disobey and begin to live their own lives. In this sense, the son bears the cross, so to speak, for the sins committed by his mother.

Much evil in the world that is done by men has its roots here, in a stiffening mother-son relation that deprived the boy for years of his vital energies, blocking his emotional flow to a point of self-forgetfulness. This is, then, the reason why these men one day explode, so to speak, for thinking of themselves 'for one time', and do something horrible, to a woman, a little girl, or an elder. And who goes to jail is always the boy, then a man, and not his mother. And that, in my humble opinion, should be changed. Women are to be made responsible for being abusive as mothers, not only men, as fathers.

My research has shown that virtually the only cultures that do not have the problem are tribal cultures, most native populations around the world.

Continuum Concept

The continuum concept is an idea relating to human development proposed by Jean Liedloff in her book *The Continuum Concept (1977/1986)*. According to Liedloff, to achieve optimal physical, mental and emotional development, human beings, especially babies, require the kind of experience to which their species adapted during the long process of their evolution.

Liedloff suggests that when certain evolutionary expectations are not met as infants and toddlers, compensation for these needs will be sought, by alternate means, throughout life, resulting in mental and social disorders.

Erotic Intelligence

Whereas formerly only the mind, and even more reductionist, the brain was considered to be the source of intelligence, today we know *that our emotions have their own unique intelligence,* that in many ways surpasses the intelligence of the mind, and that our erotic emotions, including our sexual desires, have their own intelligence as well. They in fact intelligently contribute to our holistic understanding of the world and reality; thus erotic intelligence is a form of cognition, and at the same time of intelligent communication.

Inner Selves

Inner Selves are energies in our psyche that form part of our total and integral wholeness. In the ideal case, they should be balanced and in harmony with each other. This means that all inner selves ideally should work in synch, as a sort of inner team. It is essential that all members of this inner team are fully awake and communicate with each other. In most people's psyche, however, the inner child is somnolent or asleep, and either the inner parent or the inner adult are hypertrophied and dominate the psyche.

While the truth about our inner selves goes back to Antiquity, the insight in modern times has been made fruitful for psychiatry through Eric Berne in 1950, the founder of *Transactional Analysis (TA)*. Eric Berne recognized three essential inner selves: *Inner Child, Inner Parent* and *Inner Adult.* In my own research and work with the inner dialogue during an Erickson hypnotherapy, I encountered the presence of additional entities such as the *Inner Controller* or *Inner Critic* as the instance in the psyche that represents the societal, cultural and moralistic values that we have internalized through education and conditioning. If the Inner Controller hijacks the psyche, we are unable to realize our love desires. In addition to these inner selves, I encountered an entity of superior wisdom that I called *Lux* and a shadow entity I called *Sad King* and which embodied repressed emotions that had turned into sadistic drives.

Inner Child

Inner Child is a psychic entity, part-personality, or psychic energy, created between our 7th and 14th year of life, and that is part of our inner triangle. Positively, the inner child energy is *primarily emotional and wistful,* predominantly creative. It is the motor of every human being's creativity. It can be said to be the creative motor, the very source energy in humans that makes that we can be spontaneous, creative and sometimes a little mad, to go beyond the limiting framework of the rational and repetitive mind. Negatively, the inner child is either mute or cataleptic so that its energy cannot manifest, or else its energy is turned upside-down which makes an inner child that is rebellious, capricious, willful or overbearing, producing the 'clochard' personality, the 'hippie', the 'anarchist', the 'eternal student' and abuser of the social system.

Inner Adult

Inner Adult is a psychic entity, part-personality or psychic energy that represents our logical thinking, our reason, our maturity. Positively, it makes for our balanced decisions, our down-to-earth attitude and our sense for daily responsibilities. Negatively, the inner adult manifests as the intellectual nerd or through emotional frigidity, cynicism or an obsession to measure human relations on a scale of reasonableness or straightness without considering the emotional dimension. The hypertrophied inner adult energy plays a major role in modern education where it results in devastating damage on the next generations' emotional integrity. The hypertrophied inner adult also produces the 'professional skeptic', the obnoxious 'total rationalist' who considers ten percent of the human nature as predominantly important, flushing the other ninety percent down the toilet!

Inner Parent

Inner Parent is a psychic entity, part-personality or psychic energy that represents our inner value standards, our moral attitudes, our caring for self and others, but negatively also our judging others, our I-know-better attitude or blunt interference into the lives of others without regard for their privacy.

The hypertrophied inner parent energy plays a dominant role in tyrannical and persecutory societal, religious and political systems. Nowadays, it plays a major role within our abuse-centered culture, in the stringently paranoid child protection industry that managed to turn international adoption down over the last two decades in almost all jurisdictions of the world.

Inner Dialogue

The inner dialogue is a technique to get in touch with our inner selves through relaxation or self-hypnosis and subsequent dialogues with one or several of our inner selves, in a state of light trance. The state of light trance can be self-induced, with no facilitator needed, and outside of a psychotherapy. The inner dialogue should ideally be fixed on paper, at least in the beginning, because the voices that come up, are very soft and writing down the dialogues helps to keep focus. The technique is also called *Voice Dialogue*, for example by Stone & Stone, in their book *Embracing Our Selves (1982)*. However, the expression could mislead novice users as the 'voices' are not really voices of course, as they are not to be heard with our ears, but something like intuitions, or flashes of intuition, or sudden precisely formulated thoughts that seem to come 'from nowhere'.

Minoan Culture

The ancient *Minoan Civilization* from Crete was one of the first highly developed human cultures with a natural focus on sensuality, beauty, free sexuality and a matriarchal worldview. Minoan culture can be said to have respected what Emerson called *spiritual laws*, and they had fully integrated the female in a partnership paradigm of living and shared responsibility. No slavery was practiced and no physical punishment for children in schools was given as an educational measure. The crime rate in that culture was very low. Their religion did not worship a male god but a series of goddesses and spirits of nature.

The low degree of violence in that culture was exemplary in history, yet this civilization was virtually raped and devoured by the cruel, slavery-practicing invader tribes. Riane Eisler, in her concise exposé of Minoan mores, culture and lifestyle as part of her book *The Chalice and the Blade (1995)*, speaks of Crete as The Essential Difference and reminds that already Plato described the Minoans as 'exceptionally peace-loving people.'

Among all the positive aspects Eisler mentions about Minoan culture, referencing many other scholars, the most striking is that this ancient culture had a well-built model of what today we call democracy. Still today, the health of the Cretan population and their wistful lifestyle is famed.

A recent demographic survey has shown that in Europe, the Cretan population is by far the healthiest one, and that cancer and heart disease rates are among the lowest in the world.

Among modern scholars, Terence McKenna and Riane Eisler stand out in their correct evaluation of the value of Minoan civilization and this culture's example status for modern peace research.

Pleasure Principle

Herbert James Campbell, a renowned English neurologist, found in twenty-five years of research a universal principle which dominates our brain: *the pleasure principle*. His book *The Pleasure Areas (1973)* represents a summery of many years of neurological research.

Campbell succeeded in demonstrating that our entire thinking and living is primarily motivated by pleasure, pleasure not only as tactile-sensuous or sexual pleasure, but also as non-sensuous, intellectual or spiritual pleasure.

With these findings, the old theoretical controversy if man was primarily a biological or a spiritual being, became obsolete. For it is in the first place our *striving for pleasure* that induces certain interests in us, that drives us to certain actions and that lets us choose certain ways.

Campbell also found that during childhood and depending on the outside stimuli we are exposed to, certain *preferred pathways* are traced in our brain, which means that specific neural connections are established that serve the information flow. The number of those connections is namely an indicator for intelligence.

The more of those preferred pathways exist in the brain of a person, the more lively appears that person, the more interested she will be in different things, and the quicker she will achieve integrating new knowledge into existing memory. High memorization, Campbell found, is namely depending on how easily new information can be added on to existing pathways of information. Logically, the more of those pathways exist, the better! Many preferred pathways make for high flexibility and the capacity to adapt easily to new circumstances.

Campbell's research indicates that the repression of pleasure that is since centuries part of our Judeo-Christian culture, has negatively infringed upon human evolution and impaired the integrity of our psychosomatic health.

Besides peace research, Campbell's findings are important for research on perception and the human memory surface. Our brain adds new information on to already existing information, most of the time, instead of forming a new pattern in the memory surface. This is how the brain, and the process of thought, works, and how this system impacts upon perception by actually per se distorting perception.

Campbell argues that our brain has developed this kind of faulty memory surface because it was enhancing human evolution as a matter of survival – while of course it has brought about millions of deficient thinkers! One of our major thinking trainers and international coaches, Edward de Bono, said the same from his own research on perception and his experience as a corporate trainer.

Quantum Physics

Quantum mechanics (QM, or quantum theory) is a physical science dealing with the behaviour of matter and energy on the scale of atoms and subatomic particles / waves. QM also forms the basis for the contemporary understanding of how very large objects such as stars and galaxies, and cosmological events such as the Big Bang, can be analyzed and explained. Quantum mechanics is the foundation of several related disciplines including condensed matter physics, quantum chemistry, molecular biology, particle physics, and electronics. The term 'quantum mechanics' was first coined by Max Born in 1924. The acceptance by the general physics community of quantum mechanics is due to its accurate prediction of the physical behaviour of systems, including systems where Newtonian mechanics fails. Even general relativity is limited in ways quantum mechanics is not, for describing systems at the atomic scale or smaller, or at very low or very high energies, or at the lowest temperatures.

Through a century of experimentation and applied science, quantum mechanical theory has proven to be very successful and practical. (Wikipedia)

Definition

Quantum Physics or quantum mechanics is a fundamental branch of theoretical physics with wide applications in experimental physics that replaces classical mechanics and classical electromagnetism at the atomic and subatomic levels.

It is the underlying mathematical framework of many fields of physics and chemistry, including condensed matter physics, atomic physics, molecular physics, computational chemistry, quantum chemistry, particle physics, and nuclear physics. Along with general relativity, quantum mechanics is one of the pillars of modern physics.

The Uncertainty Principle

The once certain basic assumptions about life, that were the pillars of Cartesian science, were replaced by uncertainty. It was through Werner Heisenberg that this often-quoted uncertainty principle was established in physics, and notoriously much to the exasperation of Albert Einstein who reportedly objected 'God does not play dice!'

Nonlocality

Another basic discovery of quantum physics is nonlocality. Nonlocality means that effects be triggered by element A in element B without element A and element B having any form of physical connection. They can in fact be light years away from each other. Nonlocality, then, is not bound to relativity, and effects therefore are not a function of the speed of the light nor any higher velocity; in other words, they are instantaneous. The term used for nonlocal effects is entanglement or quantum entanglement. An alternative explanation was given by Rupert Sheldrake who explains nonlocal effects by morphic resonance.

Quantum physics has been my light of hope since more than a decade. It has given me right in all my childhood intuitions, and in my violent reject of the arrogant ignorance that was sold by our science teachers as the only truth existing in the cosmos.

Extrapolating this personal experience I have come to tell children to actively resist being raped by educational systems, that until today have never understood the human brain, and therefore do not know how to properly educate a child for acquiring a stable basis of viable knowledge that later can be used in real life. Einstein knew why he dropped out of all schools and universities, and Picasso as well; there is a long list to be made of other geniuses who did the same.

Quantum physics was for me something like a heavenly punishment for all those idiot science teachers with their ignorant assumptions about life and their eternal neurosis, who bury our lively and moving children in graves called schools, thereby transforming them into living mummies.

Quantum physics with all its apparent paradoxes has for me a direct connection with the Divine in that it forces the conditioned human spirit to relax and sit back in front of the true mystery of life, and let God. Quantum physics also has something of the Hindu God Shiva, the Destroyer, in that it has destroyed the hubris of many make-belief scientists, leading all of us toward renewed humility in front of the immense intelligence that is behind Creation. I think all these paradoxes that quantum physics so abundantly serves us are the result of the moron intellectual assumptions that traditional modern science was putting up as 'eternal principles of living' but that in fact have little to do with the object of observation, that is, nature. And that is why they eventually are turning out as what they are: projections upon nature, not the outcome of observation of nature.

(See more about Quantum Physics in *Walter's Encyclopedia, Academic Edition (2010)*.

Sadism

Sadism is a blockage of the natural *emotional flow* through a predominantly moralistic or puritanical education, often accompanied by physical punishment, which leads to a repression of the natural streaming of the hot and melting sexual energy and as a result, to *demonic emotions*, and violence, because the naturally deep sexual discharge becomes shallow or even is inhibited.

As a result, the naturally hot and tender sexual feelings are disintegrated and distorted into a *compulsion for sex* targeting at strong explosive sexual discharge, as a matter of abreacting an urge, instead of embracing a mate.

Sexual discharge in fact temporarily alleviates the fear armor but tends to entangle the person, who is more or less unconscious of the affliction, long-term in sexual aggression, assault and generally a bullying, racketing or abasing behavior, that degrades and dehumanizes the mate to a passive dummy.

Sadism was badly understood before Wilhelm Reich's in-depth research on the sexual orgasm revealed that the natural sexual drive is by no means aggressive or compulsive, but controlled by empathy and love for the sexual mate. Only in sadism, which is a distortion of the natural emotional and sexual setup, this empathy tends to be overridden by an overwhelming longing for egocentric, and power-ridden, satisfaction virtually on the back, and to the detriment, of the sexual mate. This is why long-term sexual sadism leads to a corruption of the personality, as the pattern for abuse then is laid also in a general manner, and the person tends to take advantage of others in the form of a habitual behavior structure, and thus becomes what is called an abuser.

But for this to happen, the pattern *must have been ingrained for long,* and the person must never have gained consciousness about it. This is rather the extreme case, as often people become aware of their sadistic needs and begin to become suspicious of the obvious violence of their sexual behavior, and then begin to look for a way out, and may seek out a minister, physician, psychiatrist or psychotherapist for advice and consultation.

Breaking the sadism pattern is greatly facilitated by being around babies and small children, and generally, when men are actively involved in taking care of things, of children, of trees, of gardens and flowers, or of cooking and cleaning the house.

Hence, the need for involving males in early child care. All these tasks are getting men in touch with their *yin* side, or *anima,* thereby helping them to overcome the macho or hero spirit that is negatively conducive to building the abuse pattern as a long-term affliction and personality trait.

For we have to see that sadism is not only an individual problem, but also a societal concern.

Our Western culture is largely sadistic and this sadism can be shown and demonstrated with many examples from the historian's or the psychohistorian's toolbox. Thus, sadism is a direct outflow and consequence of centuries if not millennia of *moralism* as a sort of emotional plague that has distorted our *emosexual* behavior structure. Our value system is deeply freedom and touch hostile and this value system was built because our deep emotions are *out of touch with our natural emosexual base structure.* This value system is against nature because it favors violence and shuns natural sexual tenderness and respectful non-violent embrace among generations, as a prolongation of necessary and health-fostering touch among all members of society.

(More on the other terms mentioned here in *Walter's Encyclopedia, Academic Edition (2010).*

Self

I need to render an account of what I understand under the notion of *self* as it's a term that is rather ambiguous, used in different ways by different people, and by different religions. To begin with, I do not share the general disdain of Buddhism for the self as a concept that isolates and suffocates human creativity in an ego-bound shell. I rather sympathize with the Hindu notion of *atman* as the Divine higher self that is considered as an outflow of the universal spirit or oversoul, *brahman.* It is in this sense that the Indian sage *Ramana Maharshi* uses the notion of self and this comes very close to my own idea of selfhood. However, my idea has been influenced also strongly by the psychology of Carl Gustav Jung. In Jungian psychology, the self is the *archetype* symbolizing the totality of the personality. It represents the striving for unity, wholeness, and integration. As such, it embraces not only the conscious but also the unconscious.

Sigmund Freud

When I first was reading *Sigmund Freud (1856-1939)*, in its German original edition, back in 1975, upon entering law school, I fully choked all and everything. And I think that more than ninety percent of all intelligent and pro-child oriented people find that it makes sense when Freud affirms the basic sexual nature of the child and infantile sexuality. But I committed a tremendous error here, because, conditioned as I was by the Western cultural denial of the child's affective, emotional and sexual complexity, I had no idea that children could have an authentic sexual life in the sense of copulating with each other, and not just in the sense of being autoerotic by practicing masturbation.

In the absence of this knowledge, Freud's theory that children's psychosexual development was a process of libidinal (erotic) identifications with first the same-sex parent (homosexual identification), and then with the other-sex parent (heterosexual identification), passing through the oral and anal stages for finally arriving at the genital stage – is an attractive surrogate for the real knowledge! And it is an attractive lie, for it justifies the existence of the holy consumer family with a child as the main stage clown who is used and abused under the pretext of his or her needs - while the reality is that it's the parents' needs that have in the first place created this psychological fairy tale – their needs for incestuous masturbations and the socially sanctified and legally imposed avoidance of the unspeakable: the gradual building of the child's autonomy through *real* erotic experience with people outside of the nuclear family.

And this *reductionism*, sadly so, is the pseudo-scientific level of today's mainstream child psychology: a surrogate for the real, a fake, and a fairy tale about child sex mythology! Freud was the avatar for what later became, and today still is, the mainstream paradigm in child psychology and education. In my *Idiot Guide to Sanity (2010)* and my *Idiot Guide to Soul Power (2010)* I retrace the building of identity and autonomy, and point to the pitfalls in the Western educational system.

One of these pitfalls is the exclusion of parameters that serve to build identity through self-knowledge, intuitive or inner knowledge, paranormal knowledge, pre-life knowledge and relational experience. The identity that is said to be the only possible one according to Western mainstream psychiatry is a *derived*, not a genuine, identity. It is derived from the parents' identities. For a boy, for example, the process will be identification with the father, as a primary homosexual identification, during the anal phase and identification with the mother, as a secondary heterosexual identification during the genital phase.

According to Freud, the so-called *Oedipus Complex* comes in at that moment in the child's psychosexual development. True identity is built, according to this theory, when the boy has successfully liquidated the oedipal complex by having developed enough aggressiveness toward the father and enough castration of his incestuous desire toward the mother at the same time. That this system is built upon the grave of child sexuality, in the sense of child-child sexual activity, is clear from the start. It was clear to Freud but he thought that a deeper yielding to the core of nature's laws would catapult Western bourgeoisie into chaos.

I have critically reviewed Freud's theory of infantile sexuality in *Walter's Encyclopedia (2010)* on my glossary entry for the term of *Oedipus Complex* and specialized publications. I came to the conclusion that Freud's scheme is detrimental to the child's building autonomy, by keeping the Western consumer child in fusional dependence on their parents, thus creating *co-dependence* and perversion, and a fake heterosexuality that covers up all the undealt-with secondary drives that are produced by forcefully impeding the child from living out their natural erotic attraction toward peers.

My wake-up call had come not from psychology, but from the side of ethnological field work and the insights I got through my studies of the human energy field, the energetic functionality of the organism and the nature of the bio-energy. It was first of all through the anthropological findings of *Bronislaw Malinowski and Margaret Mead* and their observations of biologically healthy child-child sexuality with the Melanesian Trobriand culture, and other tribal cultures, that brought about a change in my regard upon child sexuality.

To conclude this rather lengthy exposé in simple terms. We have two ways to create a new reality, by recognizing the child's affective, emotional and sexual complexity and high bioenergetic charge, and by creating new and comprehensive forms of child-rearing:

> ▸ by confining the child in an oedipal triangle within the nuclear family, depriving them of non-incestuous erotic relations, and artificially raising their gerontophilic eroticism, while projecting this eroticism exclusively upon the child's own parents, thereby creating a striking conflict within the child's psychosomatic setup with the result of violence;

or

> ▸ by transforming mainstream culture and granting children their own domain of intimacy, outside of the parent's embrace, and allowing the child to live their affective, emotional and sexual complexity in freedom, thus helping the child to build true autonomy and self-reliance, with the result of world peace.

To summarize, Sigmund Freud has significantly contributed to consolidating what I call *Oedipal Culture*, to a point to have prepared the subtle ideological soil for *postmodern international consumer culture.* Freud has less significantly contributed to helping the modern child consolidating their natural quest for autonomy and self-reliance, and their birthright for an unobserved realm of intimacy, outside of the jovially persecutory parental and educational embrace, if not to be kept save from the Kindergarten regime of slave-puppets to their culturally perverted and schizoid parents and educators.[15] I have reviewed Freud's *Oedipus Complex* theory in my *Idiot Guide to Love (2010)* and my *Idiot Guide to Sanity (2010)*.

---

[15] See: Sigmund Freud, *Collected Writings (1924)*.

BIBLIOGRAPHY

Contextual Bibliography

Abrams, Jeremiah (Ed.)
Reclaiming the Inner Child
New York: Tarcher/Putnam, 1990

Die Befreiung des Inneren Kindes
Die Wiederentdeckung unserer ursprünglichen kreativen Persönlichkeit
und ihre zentrale Bedeutung für unser Erwachsenwerden
München: Scherz Verlag, 1993

Appleton, Matthew
A Free Range Childhood
Self-Regulation at Summerhill School
Foundation for Educational Renewal, 2000

Summerhill
Kindern ihre Kindheit zurückgeben
Demokratie und Selbstregulierung in der Erziehung
Hohengehren: Schneider Verlag, 2003

Arcas, Gérald, Dr
Guérir le corps par l'hypnose et l'auto-hypnose
Paris: Sand, 1997

Ariès, Philippe
L'enfant et la famille sous l'Ancien Régime
Paris, Seuil, 1975

Centuries of Childhood
New York: Vintage Books, 1962

Geschichte der Kindheit
Frankfurt/M: DTV, 1998

Arntz, William & Chasse, Betsy

What the Bleep Do We Know
20th Century Fox, 2005 (DVD)

Down The Rabbit Hole Quantum Edition
20th Century Fox, 2006 (3 DVD Set)

Bleep
An der Schnittstelle von Spiritualität und Wissenschaft
Verblüffende Erkenntnisse und Anstösse zum Weiterdenken
Berlin: Vak Verlag, 2007

Bachelard, Gaston

The Poetics of Reverie
Translated by Daniel Russell
Boston: Beacon Press, 1971

Poetik des Raumes
Frankfurt/M: Fischer Verlag, 2001

Bachofen, Johann Jakob

Gesammelte Werke, Band II
Das Mutterrecht
Basel: Benno Schwabe & Co., 1948
Erstveröffentlichung im Jahre 1861

Balter, Michael

The Goddess and the Bull
Catalhoyuk, An Archaeological Journey
to the Dawn of Civilization
New York: Free Press, 2006

Bandler, Richard

Get the Life You Want
The Secrets to Quick and Lasting Life Change
With Neuro-Linguistic Programming
Deerfield Beach, Fl: HCl, 2008

Bettelheim, Bruno

A Good Enough Parent
New York: A. Knopf, 1987

The Uses of Enchantment
New York: Vintage Books, 1989

Kinder brauchen Märchen
Frankfurt/M: DTV, 2002

Block, Peter

Stewardship
Choosing Service Over Self-Interest
San Francisco: Berrett-Koehler, 1996

Blofeld, J.

The Book of Changes
A New Translation of the Ancient Chinese I Ching
New York: E.P. Dutton, 1965

Blum, Ralph H. & Laughan, Susan

The Healing Runes
Tools for the Recovery of Body, Mind, Heart & Soul
New York: St. Martin's Press, 1995

Boadalla, David

Wilhelm Reich, Leben und Werk
Frankfurt/M: Fischer, 1980

Bohm, David

Wholeness and the Implicate Order
London: Routledge, 2002

Die implizite Ordnung
Grundlagen eines dynamischen Holismus
München: Goldmann Wilhelm, 1989

Thought as a System
London: Routledge, 1994

Quantum Theory
London: Dover Publications, 1989

La plénitude de l'univers
Paris: Rocher, 1992

Branden, Nathaniel

How to Raise Your Self-Esteem
New York: Bantam, 1987

Die 6 Säulen des Selbstwertgefühls
Erfolgreich und zufrieden durch ein starkes Selbst
München: Piper Verlag, 2009

Butler-Bowden, Tom

50 Success Classics
Winning Wisdom for Work & Life From 50 Landmark Books
London: Nicholas Brealey Publishing, 2004

50 Klassiker des Erfolgs
Die wichtigsten Werke von Kenneth Blanchard, Warren Buffet,
Andrew Carnegie, Stephen R. Covey, Spencer Johnson, Benjamin
Franklin, Napoleon Hill, Nelson Mandela, Anthony Robbins,
Brian Tracy, Sun Tsu, Jack Welch und vielen anderen
Frankfurt/M: MVG Verlag, 2005

Buxton, Richard

The Complete World of Greek Mythology
London: Thames & Hudson, 2007

Boldt, Laurence G.

Zen and the Art of Making a Living
A Practical Guide to Creative Career Design
New York: Penguin Arkana, 1993

How to Find the Work You Love
New York: Penguin Arkana, 1996

Zen Soup
Tasty Morsels of Zen Wisdom From Great Minds East & West
New York: Penguin Arkana, 1997

The Tao of Abundance
Eight Ancient Principles For Abundant Living
New York: Penguin Arkana, 1999

Das Tao der Fülle
Vom Reichtum, der uns glücklich macht
Mittelberg: Joy Verlag, 2001

Campbell, Herbert James

The Pleasure Areas
London: Eyre Methuen Ltd., 1973

Der Irrtum mit der Seele
München: Scherz Verlag, 1973

Les principes du plaisir
Paris: Stock, 1974

Campbell, Joseph

The Hero With A Thousand Faces
Princeton: Princeton University Press, 1973
(Bollingen Series XVII)
London: Orion Books, 1999

Der Heros in Tausend Gestalten
München: Insel Verlag, 2009

Occidental Mythology
Princeton: Princeton University Press, 1973
(Bollingen Series XVII)
New York: Penguin Arkana, 1991

The Masks of God
Oriental Mythology
New York: Penguin Arkana, 1992
Originally published 1962

Mythologie des Ostens
Die Masken Gottes Bd. 2
Basel: Sphinx Verlag, 1996

The Power of Myth
With Bill Moyers
ed. by Sue Flowers
New York: Anchor Books, 1988

Die Kraft der Mythen
Düsseldorf: Patmos Verlag, 2007

Capacchione, Lucia

The Power of Your Other Hand
North Hollywood, CA: Newcastle Publishing, 1988

Capra, Bernt Amadeus

Mindwalk
A Film for Passionate Thinkers
Based Upon Fritjof Capra's *The Turning Point*
New York: Triton Pictures, 1990

Capra, Fritjof

The Turning Point
Science, Society And The Rising Culture
New York: Simon & Schuster, 1987
Original Author Copyright, 1982

Wendezeit
Bausteine für ein neues Weltbild
München: Droemer Knaur, 2004

Le temps du changement
Science, société et nouvelle culture
Paris: Rocher, 1994

The Tao of Physics
An Exploration of the Parallels Between Modern
Physics and Eastern Mysticism
New York: Shambhala Publications, 2000
(New Edition) Originally published in 1975

Das Tao der Physik
Die Konvergenz von westlicher Wissenschaft und östlicher Philosophie
Neue und erweiterte Auflage
München: O.W. Barth bei Scherz, 2000
Ursprünglich erschienen 1975 bei Droemersche Verlagsanstalt
in Hamburg

Le tao de la physique
Paris: Sand & Tchou, 1994

The Web of Life
A New Scientific Understanding of Living Systems
New York: Doubleday, 1997
Author Copyright 1996

Lebensnetz
Ein neues Verständnis der lebendigen Welt
München: Scherz Verlag, 1999

The Hidden Connections
Integrating The Biological, Cognitive And Social
Dimensions Of Life Into A Science Of Sustainability
New York: Doubleday, 2002

Verborgene Zusammenhänge
München: Scherz, 2002

Steering Business Toward Sustainability
New York: United Nations University Press, 1995

Uncommon Wisdom
Conversations with Remarkable People
New York: Bantam, 1989

The Science of Leonardo
Inside the Mind of the Great Genius of the Renaissance
New York: Anchor Books, 2008
New York: Bantam Doubleday, 2007 (First Publishing)

Chopra, Deepak

Creating Affluence
The A-to-Z Steps to a Richer Life
New York: Amber-Allen Publishing (2003)

Synchrodestiny
Discover the Power of Meaningful Coincidence to Manifest Abundance
Audio Book / CD
Niles, IL: Nightingale-Conant, 2006

The Seven Spiritual Laws of Success
A Practical Guide to the Fulfillment of Your Dreams
Audio Book / CD
New York: Amber-Allen Publishing (2002)

Die Sieben Geistigen Gesetze des Erfolgs
Berlin: Ullstein Verlag, 2004

The Spontaneous Fulfillment of Desire
Harnessing the Infinite Power of Coincidence
New York: Random House Audio, 2003

Covey, Stephen R.
The 7 Habits of Highly Effective People
Powerful Lessons in Personal Change
New York: Free Press, 2004
15th Anniversary Edition
First Published in 1989

Die 7 Wege zur Effektivität
Prinzipien für persönlichen und beruflichen Erfolg
Offenbach: Gabal Verlag, 2009

The 8th Habit
From Effectiveness to Greatness
London: Simon & Schuster, 2004

Der 8. Weg
Von der Effektivität zur wahren Grösse
6. Auflage
Offenbach: Gabal Verlag, 2006

Covitz, Joel
Emotional Child Abuse
The Family Curse
Boston: Sigo Press, 1986

De Bono, Edward

The Use of Lateral Thinking
New York: Penguin, 1967

The Mechanism of Mind
New York: Penguin, 1969

Sur/Petition
London: HarperCollins, 1993

Tactics
London: HarperCollins, 1993
First published in 1985

Taktiken und Strategien erfolgreicher Menschen
Frankfurt/M: MVG Verlag, 1995

Serious Creativity
Using the Power of Lateral Thinking to Create New Ideas
London: HarperCollins, 1996

Deleuze, Gilles, Guattari, Felix

L'Anti-Oedipe
Capitalisme et Schizophrénie
Nouvelle Édition Augmentée
Paris: Éditions de Minuit, 1973

DeMause, Lloyd

The History of Childhood
New York, 1974

Foundations of Psychohistory
New York: Creative Roots, 1982

Dürckheim, Karlfried Graf

Hara: The Vital Center of Man
Rochester: Inner Traditions, 2004

Hara
Die Erdmitte des Menschen
Neuausgabe
München: O.W. Barth bei Scherz, 2005

Zen and Us
New York: Penguin Arkana 1991

The Call for the Master
New York: Penguin Books, 1993

Absolute Living
The Otherworldly in the World and the Path to Maturity
New York: Penguin Arkana, 1992

The Way of Transformation
Daily Life as a Spiritual Exercise
London: Allen & Unwin, 1988

Der Alltag als Übung
Vom Weg der Verwandlung
Bern: Huber, 2008

The Japanese Cult of Tranquility
London: Rider, 1960

Kultur der Stille
Frankfurt/M: Weltz Verlag, 1997

Eisler, Riane
The Chalice and the Blade
Our history, Our future
San Francisco: Harper & Row, 1995

Kelch und Schwert, Unsere Geschichte, unsere Zukunft
Weibliches und männliches Prinzip in der Geschichte
Freiburg: Arbor Verlag, 2005

Sacred Pleasure: Sex, Myth and the Politics of the Body
New Paths to Power and Love
San Francisco: Harper & Row, 1996

The Partnership Way
New Tools for Living and Learning
With David Loye
Brandon, VT: Holistic Education Press, 1998

The Real Wealth of Nations
Creating a Caring Economics
San Francisco: Berrett-Koehler Publishers, 2008

Eliade, Mircea

Shamanism
Archaic Techniques of Ecstasy
New York: Pantheon Books, 1964

Ellis, Havelock

Sexual Inversion
Republished
New York: University Press of the Pacific, 2001
Originally published in 1897

Analysis of the Sexual Impulse
Love and Pain
The Sexual Impulse in Women
Republished
New York: University Press of the Pacific, 2001
Originally published in 1903

The Dance of Life
New York: Greenwood Press Reprint Edition, 1973
Originally published in 1923

Elwin, V.

The Muria and their Ghotul
Bombay: Oxford University Press, 1947

Erickson, Milton H.

My Voice Will Go With You
The Teaching Tales of Milton H. Erickson
by Sidney Rosen (Ed.)
New York: Norton & Co., 1991

Complete Works 1.0, CD-ROM
New York: Milton H. Erickson Foundation, 2001

Erikson, Erik H.

Childhood and Society
New York: Norton, 1993
First published in 1950

Farson, Richard

Birthrights
A Bill of Rights for Children
Macmillan, New York, 1974

Fensterhalm, Herbert

Don't Say Yes When You Want to Say No
With Jean Bear
New York: Dell, 1980

Freud, Sigmund

Three Essays on the Theory of Sexuality
in: The Standard Edition of the Complete Psychological
Works of Sigmund Freud
London: Hogarth Press, 1953-54
Vol. 7, pp. 130 ff
(first published in 1905)

Drei Abhandlungen zur Sexualtheorie
Frankfurt/M: Fischer, 1991

The Interpretation of Dreams
New York: Avon, Reissue Edition, 1980

and in: The Standard Edition of the Complete Psychological
Works of Sigmund Freud
(24 Volumes) ed. by James Strachey
New York: W. W. Norton & Company, 1976

Die Traumdeutung
Frankfurt/M: Fischer, 2005

Totem and Taboo
New York: Routledge, 1999
Originally published in 1913

Totem und Tabu
Einige Übereinstimmungen im Seelenleben der Wilden
und der Neurotiker
Frankfurt/M: Fischer Verlag, 1972

Goleman, Daniel

Emotional Intelligence
New York, Bantam Books, 1995

EQ. Emotionale Intelligenz
München: DTV Verlag, 1997

Goswami, Amit

The Self-Aware Universe
How Consciousness Creates the Material World
New York: Tarcher/Putnam, 1995

Das Bewusste Universum
Wie Bewusstsein die materielle Welt erschafft
Stuttgart: Lüchow Verlag, 2007

Greene, Liz

The Mythic Journey
With Juliet Sharman-Burke
The Meaning of Myth as a Guide for Life
New York: Simon & Schuster (Fireside), 2000

Die Mythische Reise
Die Bedeutung der Mythen als ein Führer durch das Leben
München: Atmosphären Verlag, 2004

Hicks, Esther and Jerry

The Amazing Power of Deliberate Intent
Living the Art of Allowing
Carlsbad, CA: Hay House, 2006

Holmes, Ernst

The Science of Mind
A Philosophy, A Faith, A Way of Life
New York: Jeremy P. Tarcher/Putnam, 1998
First Published in 1938

Houston, Jean

The Possible Human
A Course in Enhancing Your Physical, Mental, and Creative Abilities
New York: Jeremy P. Tarcher/Putnam, 1982

Hunt, Valerie

Infinite Mind
Science of the Human Vibrations of Consciousness
Malibu, CA: Malibu Publishing, 2000

Jackson, Stevi

Childhood and Sexuality
New York: Blackwell, 1982

Jung, Carl Gustav

Archetypen
München: DTV Verlag, 2001

Archetypes of the Collective Unconscious
in: The Basic Writings of C.G. Jung
New York: The Modern Library, 1959, 358-407

Collected Works
New York, 1959

Dialectique du moi et de l'inconscient
Paris, Gallimard, 1991

On the Nature of the Psyche
in: The Basic Writings of C.G. Jung
New York: The Modern Library, 1959, 47-133

Psychological Types
Collected Writings, Vol. 6
Princeton: Princeton University Press, 1971

Psychologie und Religion
München: DTV Verlag, 2001

Psychology and Religion
in: The Basic Writings of C.G. Jung
New York: The Modern Library, 1959, 582-655

Religious and Psychological Problems of Alchemy
in: The Basic Writings of C.G. Jung
New York: The Modern Library, 1959, 537-581

Symbol und Libido
Freiburg: Walter Verlag, 1987

Synchronizität, Akausalität und Okkultismus
Frankfurt/M: DTV, 2001

The Basic Writings of C.G. Jung
New York: The Modern Library, 1959

The Development of Personality
Collected Writings, Vol. 17
Princeton: Princeton University Press, 1954

The Meaning and Significance of Dreams
Boston: Sigo Press, 1991

The Myth of the Divine Child
in: Essays on A Science of Mythology
Princeton, N.J.: Princeton University Press Bollingen
Series XXII, 1969. (With Karl Kerenyi)

Traum und Traumdeutung
München: DTV Verlag, 2001

Two Essays on Analytical Psychology
Collected Writings, Vol. 7
Princeton: Princeton University Press, 1972
First published by Routledge & Kegan Paul, Ltd., 1953

Zur Psychologie westlicher und östlicher Religion
Fünfte Auflage
Olten: Walter Verlag, 1988

Krishnamurti, J.

Freedom From The Known
San Francisco: Harper & Row, 1969

The First and Last Freedom
San Francisco: Harper & Row, 1975

Education and the Significance of Life
London: Victor Gollancz, 1978

Commentaries on Living
First Series
London: Victor Gollancz, 1985

Commentaries on Living
Second Series
London: Victor Gollancz, 1986

Krishnamurti's Journal
London: Victor Gollancz, 1987

Krishnamurti's Notebook
London: Victor Gollancz, 1986

Beyond Violence
London: Victor Gollancz, 1985

Beginnings of Learning
New York: Penguin, 1986

The Penguin Krishnamurti Reader
New York: Penguin, 1987

On God
San Francisco: Harper & Row, 1992

On Fear
San Francisco: Harper & Row, 1995

The Essential Krishnamurti
San Francisco: Harper & Row, 1996

The Ending of Time
With Dr. David Bohm
San Francisco: Harper & Row, 1985

Leonard, George, Murphy, Michael

The Live We Are Given
A Long Term Program for Realizing the
Potential of Body, Mind, Heart and Soul
New York: Jeremy P. Tarcher/Putnam, 1984

Liedloff, Jean

Continuum Concept
In Search of Happiness Lost
New York: Perseus Books, 1986
First published in 1977

Auf der Suche nach dem verlorenen Glück
Gegen die Zerstörung der Glücksfähigkeit in der frühen Kindheit
München: C.H. Beck Verlag, 2006

Lowen, Alexander

Angst vor dem Leben
Über den Ursprung seelischen Leides und den Weg
zu einem reicheren Dasein
München: Goldmann Wilhelm, 1989

Bioenergetics
New York: Coward, McGoegham 1975

Bioenergetik
Therapie der Seele durch Arbeit mit dem Körper
Berlin: Rowohlt, 2008

Depression and the Body
The Biological Basis of Faith and Reality
New York: Penguin, 1992

Fear of Life
New York: Bioenergetic Press, 2003

Honoring the Body
The Autobiography of Alexander Lowen
New York: Bioenergetic Press, 2004

Joy
The Surrender to the Body and to Life
New York: Penguin, 1995

Love and Orgasm
New York: Macmillan, 1965

Love, Sex and Your Heart
New York: Bioenergetics Press, 2004

Narcissism: Denial of the True Self
New York: Macmillan, Collier Books, 1983

Narzissmus
Die Verleugnung des wahren Selbst
München: Goldmann Wilhelm, 1992

Pleasure: A Creative Approach to Life
New York: Bioenergetics Press, 2004
First published in 1970

The Language of the Body
Physical Dynamics of Character Structure
New York: Bioenergetics Press, 2006

Maharshi, Ramana

The Collected Works of Ramana Maharshi
New York: Sri Ramanasramam, 2002

The Essential Teachings of Ramana Maharshi
A Visual Journey
New York: Inner Directions Publishing, 2002
by Matthew Greenblad

Sei was du bist!
München: O.W. Barth, 2001

Nan Yar? Wer bin ich?
München: Kamphausen, 2002

Malinowski, Bronislaw

Crime und Custom in Savage Society
London: Kegan, 1926

Sex and Repression in Savage Society
London: Kegan, 1927

The Sexual Life of Savages in North West Melanesia
New York: Halycon House, 1929

Das Geschlechtsleben der Wilden in Nordwest-Melanesien
Liebe, Ehe und Familienleben bei den Eingeborenen der
Trobriand Inseln, Britisch-Neuguinea
Eschborn: Klotz Verlag, 2005

McKenna, Terence
The Archaic Revival
San Francisco: Harper & Row, 1992

Food of The Gods
A Radical History of Plants, Drugs and Human Evolution
London: Rider, 1992

Die Speisen der Götter
Berlin: Synergia/Syntropia, 1996

The Invisible Landscape
Mind Hallucinogens and the I Ching
New York: HarperCollins, 1993
(With Dennis McKenna)

True Hallucinations
Being the Account of the Author's Extraordinary
Adventures in the Devil's Paradise
New York: Fine Communications, 1998

McLeod, Kembrew
Freedom of Expression
Resistance and Repression in the Age of Intellectual Property
Minneapolis, MN: University of Minnesota Press, 2007

McNiff, Shaun

Art as Medicine
Boston: Shambhala, 1992

Art as Therapy
Creating a Therapy of the Imagination
Boston/London: Shambhala, 1992

Trust the Process
An Artist's Guide to Letting Go
New York: Shambhala Publications, 1998

McTaggart, Lynne

The Field
The Quest for the Secret Force of the Universe
New York: Harper & Collins, 2002

Mead, Margaret

Sex and Temperament in Three Primitive Societies
New York, 1935

Miller, Alice

Four Your Own Good
Hidden Cruelty in Child-Rearing and the Roots of Violence
New York: Farrar, Straus & Giroux, 1983

Am Anfang war Erziehung
München: Suhrkamp Verlag, 2008
Erstmals publiziert im Jahre 1986

Pictures of a Childhood
New York: Farrar, Straus & Giroux, 1986

The Drama of the Gifted Child
In Search for the True Self
translated by Ruth Ward
New York: Basic Books, 1996

Das Drama des Begabten Kindes
Und die Suche nach dem wahren Selbst
München: Suhrkamp Verlag, 1983

Der gemiedene Schlüssel
München: Suhrkamp, 2007

Das verbannte Wissen
Frankfurt/M: Suhrkamp, 1988

Thou Shalt Not Be Aware
Society's Betrayal of the Child
New York: Noonday, 1998

Du Sollst Nicht Merken
Variationen über das Paradies-Thema
Neuauflage
München: Suhrkamp, 2005

The Political Consequences of Child Abuse
in: The Journal of Psychohistory 26, 2 (Fall 1998)

Montagu, Ashley

Touching
The Human Significance of the Skin
New York: Harper & Row, 1978

Körperkontakt
8. Auflage
Stuttgart: Klett/Cotta, 1995

Montessori, Maria

The Absorbent Mind
Reprint Edition
New York: Buccaneer Books, 1995
First published in 1973

Moore, Thomas

Care of the Soul
A Guide for Cultivating Depth and Sacredness in Everyday Life
New York: Harper & Collins, 1994

Die Seele Lieben
Tiefe und Spiritualität im täglichen Leben
München: Droemer Knaur, 1995

Murphy, Joseph

The Power of Your Subconscious Mind
West Nyack, N.Y.: Parker, 1981, N.Y.: Bantam, 1982
Originally published in 1962

Die Macht Ihres Unterbewusstseins
München: Hugendubel, 2000

La puissance de votre subconscient
Genève: Ramón Keller, 1967

The Miracle of Mind Dynamics
New York: Prentice Hall, 1964

Miracle Power for Infinite Riches
West Nyack, N.Y.: Parker, 1972

The Amazing Laws of Cosmic Mind Power
West Nyack, N.Y.: Parker, 1973

Secrets of the I Ching
West Nyack, N.Y.: Parker, 1970

Think Yourself Rich
Use the Power of Your Subconscious Mind to Find True Wealth
Revised by Ian D. McMahan, Ph.D.
Paramus, NJ: Reward Books, 2001

Das Erfolgsbuch
Wie sie alles im Leben erreichen können
Hamburg: Heyne Verlag, 2002

Wahrheiten die ihr Leben verändern
Dr. Joseph Murphys Vermächtnis
München: Hugendubel, 1996

Murphy, Michael

The Future of the Body
Explorations into the Further Evolution of Human Nature
New York: Jeremy P. Tarcher/Putnam, 1992

Der Quanten-Mensch
München: Ludwig Verlag, 1996

Myers, Tony Pearce

The Soul of Creativity
Insights into the Creative Process
Novato, CA: New World Library, 1999

Narby, Jeremy

The Cosmic Serpent
DNA and the Origins of Knowledge
New York: J. P. Tarcher, 1999

Die Kosmische Schlange
Auf den Pfaden der Schamanen zu den Ursprüngen modernen Wissens
Stuttgart: Klett-Cotta, 2007

Nau, Erika

Self-Awareness Through Huna
Virginia Beach: Donning, 1981

Selbstbewusst durch Huna
Die magische Weisheit Hawaiis
2. Auflage
Basel: Sphinx Verlag, 1989

Ostrander, Sheila & Schroeder, Lynn

Superlearning 2000
New York: Delacorte Press, 1994

Superlearning
Die revolutionäre Lernmethode
München: Scherz Verlag, 1979

Supermemory
New York: Carroll & Graf, 1991

SuperMemory
Der Weg zum optimalen Gedächtnis
München: Goldmann, 1996

Pearce, John A. II and Robinson B. Jr.

Strategic Management
Formulation, Implementation and Control
Tenth Edition
New York: McGraw-Hill, 2007

Pearce Myers, Tony (Editor)

The Soul of Creativity
Insights into the Creative Process
Novato: New World Library, 1999

Pert, Candace B.

Molecules of Emotion
The Science Behind Mind-Body Medicine
New York: Scribner, 2003

Petrash, Jack

Understanding Waldorf Education
Teaching from the Inside Out
London: Floris Books, 2003

Porteous, Hedy S.

Sex and Identity
Your Child's Sexuality
Indianapolis: Bobbs-Merrill, 1972

Radin, Dean

The Conscious Universe
The Scientific Truth of Psychic Phenomena
San Francisco: Harper & Row, 1997

Entangled Minds
Extrasensory Experiences in a Quantum Reality
New York: Paraview Pocket Books, 2006

Raknes, Ola

Wilhelm Reich and Orgonomy
Oslo: Universitetsforlaget, 1970

Wilhelm Reich und die Orgonomie
Eine Einführung in die Wissenschaft von der Lebensenergie
Frankfurt/M: Nexus, 1983

Reich, Wilhelm

Children of the Future
On the Prevention of Sexual Pathology
New York: Farrar, Straus & Giroux, 1983
First published in 1950

Selected Writings
An Introduction to Orgonomy
New York: Farrar, Straus & Giroux, 1973

The Mass Psychology of Fascism
New York: Farrar, Straus & Giroux, 1970
Originally published in 1933

Robbins, Anthony

Awaken The Giant Within
New York: Simon & Schuster, 1991

Unlimited Power
The New Science of Personal Achievement
New York: Free Press, 1997

Roberts, Jane

The Nature of Personal Reality
New York: Amber-Allen Publishing, 1994
First published in 1974

Die Natur der Persönlichen Realität
Ein neues Bewusstsein als Quelle der Kreativität
München: Kailash Verlag, 2007

The Nature of the Psyche
Its Human Expression
New York, Amber-Allen Publishing, 1996
First published in 1979

Die Natur der Psyche
Ihr menschlicher Ausdruck in Kreativität, Liebe, Sexualität
Genf: Ariston Verlag, 1985

Die Natur der Psyche
Ihr menschlicher Ausdruck in Kreativität, Liebe, Sexualität
München: Kailash Verlag, 2008

Rothschild & Wolf

Children of the Counterculture
New York: Garden City, 1976

Rousseau, Jean-Jacques

Émile ou de l'Éducation, 1762
Reprint, Paris: Garnier, 1964

The Social Contract
And Later Political Writings
Cambridge, MA.: Cambridge University Press, 1997

Rudhyar, Dane

Astrology of Personality
A Reformulation of Astrological Concepts and Ideals in
Terms of Contemporary Psychology and Philosophy
New York: Aurora Press, 1990

An Astrological Triptych
Gifts of the Spirit, The Way Through, and The Illumined Road
New York: Aurora Press, 1991

Astrological Mandala
New York: Vintage Books, 1994

L'astrologie de la transformation
Paris: Rocher, 1984

Ruiz, Don Miguel

The Four Agreements
A Practical Guide to Personal Freedom
San Rafael, CA: Amber Allen Publishing, 1997

The Mastery of Love
A Practical Guide to the Art of Relationship
San Rafael, CA: Amber Allen Publishing, 1999

The Voice of Knowledge
A Practical Guide to Inner Peace
San Rafael, CA: Amber Allen Publishing, 2004

Ruperti, Alexander

Cycles of Becoming
The Planetary Pattern of Growth
New York: CRCS Publications, 1978

Sheldrake, Rupert

A New Science of Life
The Hypothesis of Morphic Resonance
Rochester: Park Street Press, 1995

Das Schöpferische Universum
Die Theorie des morphogenetischen Feldes
Neue und erweiterte Auflage
Berlin: Ullstein, 2009

Shone, Ronald

Creative Visualization
Using Imagery and Imagination for Self-Transformation
New York: Destiny Books, 1998

Tolle, Eckhart

The Power of Now
A Guide to Spiritual Enlightenment
Novato, CA: New World Library, 2004

Jetzt! Die Kraft der Gegenwart
Ein Leitfaden zum spirituellen Erwachen
Bielefeld: Kamphausen Verlag, 2000

A New Earth
Awakening to Your Life's Purpose
New York: Michael Joseph (Penguin), 2005

Eine neue Erde
Bewusstseinssprung anstelle von Selbstzerstörung
München: Goldmann, 2005

Wild, Leon D.

The Runes Workbook
A Step-by-Step Guide to Learning the Wisdom of the Staves
San Diego: Thunder Bay Press, 2004

Williams, Strephon Kaplan

Dreams and Spiritual Growth
With Patricia H. Berne and Louis M. Savary
New York: Paulist Press, 1984

Durch Traumarbeit zum eigenen Selbst
Die Jung-Senoi Methode
Interlaken: Ansata Verlag, 1987

Dream Cards
Understand Your Dreams and Enrich Your Life
New York: Simon & Schuster (Fireside), 1991

Wolf, Fred Alan

Taking the Quantum Leap
The New Physics for Nonscientists
New York: Harper & Row, 1989

Der Quantensprung ist keine Hexerei
Frankfurt/M: Fischer Verlag, 1990

Parallel Universes
New York: Simon & Schuster, 1990

The Dreaming Universe
A Mind-Expanding Journey into the Realm
Where Psyche and Physics Meet
New York: Touchstone, 1995

The Eagle's Quest
A Physicist Finds the Scientific Truth At the Heart of the Shamanic World
New York: Touchstone, 1997

Die Physik der Träume
Frankfurt/M: DTV Verlag, 1997

Mind into Matter
A New Alchemy of Science and Spirit
New York: Moment Point Press, 2000

Zyman, Sergio

The End of Marketing as We Know It
New York: HarperCollins, 2000

Das Ende der Marketing Mythen
Erfolgsrezepte des Aya-Cola für Umsatz und Profit
Berlin: Econ Verlag, 2000

FROM THE SAME AUTHOR

A Bibliography

You can search publications from here:
http://ipublica.com/books/

For audio books and music, you can start here:
http://ipublica.com/audio/

All paperbacks, audio downloads, audio book compact discs, music downloads and music compact discs, as well as Kindle books, are referenced on the site.

For free podcasts search iTunes under my author name.

For quoting my publications, please use the following form:
Pierre F. Walter, [Title]: [Subtitle], Newark: Sirius-C Media Galaxy LLC, 2011

Web Presence

Pierre F. Walter on the Web

Sites

http://authoryourlife.com

http://ipublica.com

http://ipublica.net

http://ipublica.org

http://ipublica.tv

Video Channels

http://youtube.com/user/ipublica

http://youtube.com/user/authoryourlife

http://vimeo.com/pierrefwalter/channels

http://ipublica.blip.tv/

http://authoryourlife.blip.tv/

http://emosexuality.blip.tv/

http://pierrefwalter.blip.tv/